The I ... rary

AUSTRALIA

Graham Houghton & Julia Wakefield

CONTENTS

M

Pacific Ocean
Timor Sea
Indian Ocean
Tasman Sea
Brisbane
Cairns
Townsville
QUEENSLAND
Sydney
AUSTRALIAN CAPITAL TERRITORY
NEW SOUTH WALES
CANBERRA
Murray River
Darling River
Melbourne
VICTORIA
TASMANIA
Hobart
Adelaide
SOUTH AUSTRALIA
Lake Eyre
Alice Springs
NORTHERN TERRITORY
Darwin
WESTERN AUSTRALIA
Derby
Broome
Port Hedland
Perth
kilometres
0
500

AUSTRALIA

Geography

Australia is an island continent almost the size of the United States of America mainland, and one and a half times the size of Western Europe. It is made from some of the oldest rock on Earth; its highest mountain at 2,228 metres is Mount Kosciusko in the Australian Alps.

The Australian Alps are part of the Great Dividing Range which stretches from Victoria in the south-east to Queensland in the north. The Dividing Range is an important factor in the environment of the eastern half of Australia. The mountains are a watershed, that is the rivers which carry the rainwater runoff flow east, or west. Those which flow eastward are short, fast-flowing and eventually run over rich floodplains into the sea. Those which flow westward run into the flat inland areas where they quickly soak into the dry desert soils, or evaporate away in the intense heat. The country to the east of the Range receives more rainfall than that on the west, and so arable farming, or crop growing, is concentrated there. The drier inland is more suited to sheep and cattle farming.

Compared with the other major land masses, Australia is low lying and flat. Vast central plains formed over millions of years as the sea, sun, wind, and rain combined to erode ancient mountains. Much of the flat inland is desert today, but at one time was much more fertile, with many lakes and marshes. Some of these old lakes survive today as salt lakes like Lake Eyre in South Australia which occasionally fills with water.

Overlooking Adelaide: beyond the hospitable coast lies harsh desert.

Thousand of kilometres of desert surround Alice Springs.

Climate and Environment

Australia experiences a variety of climates. The temperate south has cool, wet winters and warm, dry summers. In the north, a tropical climate prevails with a warm, dry season and a hot, wet season. The extreme north-west experiences the edge of the monsoon systems, while the mountains of the south-east attract seasonal snow to form some of the largest Alpine snowfields in the world.

Most of Australia is hot and dry with vast expanses of sandy desert or gibber stone plains giving way to shrub savannah or mallee scrub. However in coastal regions, environments range from tropical rain forest along the north-east and north, to pastural lands and schlerophyll forest in the east and the south-east, and to alpine country in the Snowy Mountains and central Tasmania.

The Franklin River, Tasmania.

Native Plants and Animals

The plants and animals of Australia have evolved in isolation from the rest of the world over millions of years and are able to survive in some of the harshest conditions on Earth. Because of that, many are unique to Australia and some represent primitive types which died out elsewhere long ago. When Europeans began to study Australia's natural history the reports which they sent back to their homelands were not believed, such as those of the Duck Billed Platypus. This creature, together with the echidna, are the only two mammals which lay eggs and yet suckle their young with milk. The platypus also has a beak, and when scientists in London first heard of it they took it to be a practical joke.

Most Australian mammals are marsupials; they carry their young in pouches instead of giving birth to a fully formed offspring like placental mammals such as humans, apes and dogs. The only other marsupials in the world originate in South America to which Australia was once joined many millions of years ago. The best known native Australian mammals are the kangaroo and the koala. Others, such as the Thylacine, or Tasmanian wolf, and the numbat, are of great scientific interest.

Koalas eat leaves for water.

The Echidna is a monotreme.

Australia prohibits the export of native animals. Many of them, particularly the birds and reptiles, are prized by collectors. The emu is featured on the Australian Coat of Arms while others, such as the lyrebird, are used as State Government Department emblems. The kookaburra and the magpie have distinctive calls and there are large numbers of hawks and eagles. Many varieties of parrots congregate in large flocks. Others, such as the brolga and cassowary, are hard to find.

Reptiles include two sorts of crocodiles, over 140 kinds of snakes and 17 species of tortoises and turtles. The monitor lizard, or goanna, is the largest lizard in Australia and is related to the giant komodo dragon. Unusual reptiles include the frilled lizard which raises a large frill around its neck to make it appear larger and thus frighten away enemies, and the stumpy tail lizard which has large scales.

First Discovery

Australia was first discovered over 60,000 years ago and has been continuously occupied ever since. The first Australians may have arrived by a land route from Papua New Guinea because at that time the sea level was lower than it is today. This meant that the sea bed between the two countries was exposed and acted as a 'bridge' between them. The first people, known to the later

Early European drawings of an Aboriginal tribe.

European arrivals as Aborigines, (Aborigine simply means 'original inhabitant'), lived in orderly tribal societies. In some parts of Australia the tribal system has been able to survive the pressures of living alongside the European system.

Tribal Life of the Australian Aborigines

Before the arrival of the Europeans the Aboriginal peoples lived by hunting and gathering. The many skills needed to maintain this lifestyle, such as tracking, tool and weapon-making, and the abilities to recognise food plants and to locate water are still in use today. The native Aboriginal religion has played a large part in the survival of the people as a whole, and remains important for their future. Their songs, stories, dance and art are all parts of their religious beliefs. Together these things have enabled the Aboriginal people to live for thousands of years in places which many people still think of as being hostile.

European Discovery and Settlement

Australia was known to Spanish and Portuguese sailors in the sixteenth century, but may have been visited even earlier by Chinese and Arab traders. The first real attempt at exploration of the area was made by Abel Tasman, a Dutch navigator of the seventeenth century. He gave the name 'New Holland' to the island continent. In 1642 he discovered the island of Tasmania which he named Van Diemen's Land. In 1688 William Dampier, a former pirate, became the first known Englishman to set foot on Australian soil. This was in the north-west of the country and he did not like what he found.

Captain Arthur Phillip arrives with the First Fleet 1788.

The Beginnings of Settlement

The father of European settlement in Australia was Captain James Cook who carried out voyages of world exploration for the British Government. In 1768 he set out in command of the ship *Endeavour* on a mission to discover the mysterious 'Southland' which had been the subject of much talk in Europe since the second century A.D. when it first appeared on a Greek map of the world. On 20 April 1770, Cook made his landfall in south-east Australia and then followed the coast northwards for nine days until he made a landing at what is now known as Botany Bay. Sailing further north, Cook's ship was damaged on a reef and he beached her for repairs near the modern settlement of Cookstown. After two months the *Endeavour* was afloat again. When Cook reached an island off Cape York, the British flag was raised and the eastern half of Australia came under the control of the British Crown for the first time. Cook named that island Possession Island. But British settlement in Australia did not begin until the arrival of the first convict fleet nearly twenty years later.

British Loss of the Americas

Transportation to the Colonies was a common form of punishment for criminals in Britain at that time and many had been sent to America. When America won its War of Independence against Britain a new convict settlement had to be found. Joseph Banks, the official botanist on Cook's *Endeavour*, suggested that Australia would be a good place for the new settlement. And so, on 13 May 1787, eleven ships sailed from England under the command of Arthur Phillip who was to become the first Governor of the new Colony.

Arrival of the First Fleet

The fleet arrived at Botany Bay on 18 January 1788 and spent eight days there before moving on to Port Jackson. Although most of the people on board were convicts, there were also free men such as sailors and marines. This first settlement grew into Australia's largest city, Sydney. The formal possession and founding of Australia is celebrated each year on Australia Day, 26 January, the date of the landing at Port Jackson.

Opening Up The New Land

As permanent settlements were being built in the small areas of known coast, many explorers explorers set off to find out more about this strange new land. Some went in search of a vast inland sea to which many believed several large rivers would lead. Others went in search of gold and other precious minerals. A number of scientific expeditions drew up maps of the country, followed rivers, and made studies of the plants and animals. Many lost their lives through starvation, thirst, or in battles with Aborigines whose lands they trespassed. In 1813 the Blue Mountains to the west of Sydney were crossed for the first time. The explorers Wentworth and Gregory led the way to the rich grazing lands of the interior which lay to the east of Sydney.

The Return of Burke and Wills to Cooper's Creek

Burke and Wills

The most famous incident involving explorers who lost their lives in the outback is that of Burke and Wills. After successfully reaching the Gulf of Carpentaria in the north they began the 2,400 kilometre trek back to Melbourne. But the expedition was badly organised and many men had left during the early stages. Those who stayed were unhappy with Burke's poor leadership. Burke refused all contact with the Aborigines, who could have saved his life. Eventually Burke and Wills both died from thirst and starvation. Of the whole expedition, only John King survived, through the help of the Aborigines he met on his travels in the North.

States and Territories

The establishment of cities allowed major, organised exploration of the inland areas to take place. These cities were sited on the coast for two reasons. First, they relied on easy access to shipping to bring supplies and needed good port facilities. Second, the pioneer farmers were confined to the narrow coastal plains because of the poor soils and lack of water inland. Sydney, founded in 1788, Hobart in 1803, Brisbane (Moreton Bay) in 1824, and the Swan River Settlement (Perth) in 1829, were all established initially as convict settlements. The entire eastern half of Australia was at first governed from New South Wales; only South Australia and Western Australia grew as individual colonies, governed by Britain, from their beginnings. Self-government was gradually given to the eastern States, the first being Tasmania, or Van Diemen's Land as it was then called, in 1825. Victoria separated from New South Wales in 1851, and Queensland in 1859. Full self-government was granted by Britain to South Australia in 1856, and to Western Australia in 1890.

Federation, the Monarchy and Government

Australian Capital Territory

Queen Elizabeth the Second is the official Head of Government and is represented in Australia by the Governor-General. The Federal Parliament meets in Canberra in the Australian Capital Territory (ACT). The ACT was given by New South Wales to the Commonwealth of Australia in 1911 and includes an area of 735 square kilometres on the coast at Jervis Bay acquired in 1915.

States and Commonwealth

Until 1901 the government of Australia was divided into the government of the various independent States. This produced a wide difference in the various laws, which made areas such as taxation and trade difficult to manage. The States agreed in the 1890s to form a united nation to be known as the Commonwealth of Australia, and to have a Federal Parliament. On 1 January 1901 the Commonwealth came into being and its first Parliament opened in Melbourne on 29 April. The Federal Parliament moved to Canberra in 1927. Nevertheless, each State still has its own legislative assembly and is responsible for providing government over services such as education, health, transport, roads, the environment and law enforcement.

The current Parliament House, Canberra, is soon to be rebuilt.

Constitution and Parlaiment

The modern Australian political system is a mixture of the American and British types. There is a written Constitution and a two house Parliament. The lower house is called the House of Representatives and the upper house is called the Senate. Both houses are elected. Voting is compulsory for all qualified adults.

Agriculture

Agriculture is known as primary industry and its produce as primary products. Because of the range of conditions that affect Australia most types of primary industry are successful somewhere. The lush coastal plains and river valleys of the East and South-east favour dairy cattle, sheep, cereals and soft fruits such as strawberries and grapes. Drier, hot areas support beef cattle, although sometimes only one head per square kilometre. Because of this, outback 'stations' often cover thousands of square kilometres, and stockmen use helicopters to round up stock! More temperate dry zones favour sheep.

In tropical, wet areas sugar cane and fruits such as pineapples and bananas grow well. Further South apples, pears, and citrus fruits are grown.

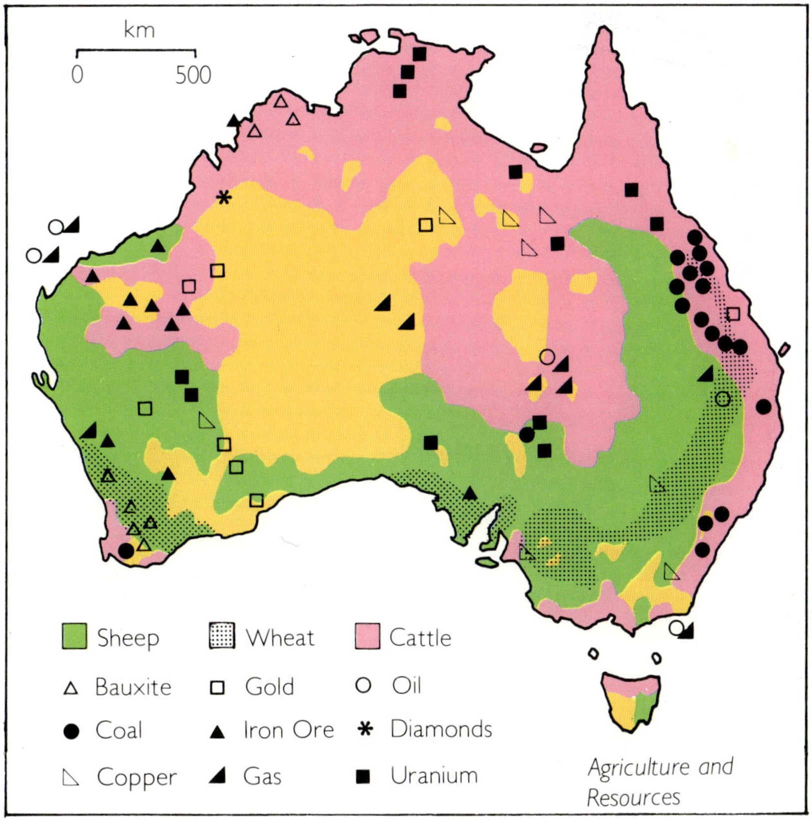

Agriculture and Resources

Coastal Eastern Australia offers lush grazing. Elsewhere the land can only feed one animal on each square kilometre!

Australia was self-supporting in food by 1795. The successful introduction of Merino sheep from Spain by John Macarthur in the late eighteenth century proved that the country had an agricultural future. Many new machines were invented in Australia in order to deal with the hard work of clearing the bush for crops and to improve production levels. The stump-jump plough was invented by Robert Smith of South Australia and was soon sold in great numbers in the United States of America as well as Australia. Mechanical shears to speed the wool harvest and improved wool presses for baling the fleeces were also developed in Australia. The rotary hoe, now used by farmers all over the world, was designed by Cliff Howard of New South Wales.

Australia exports many of its primary products which have a reputation for being of the best quality. Wool is sold to Japan and beef to the United States of America. Cereals such as wheat and barley are another important export to many parts of the world, including the USSR. The total value of farm produce in Australia is about twelve billion dollars each year.

Natural Resources

Australia is rich in most of the minerals needed for industry. Since the earliest days of European settlement prospectors have searched the country for anything from gold and diamonds to coal and rare earths. The gold rushes of the nineteenth century brought thousands of new settlers in search of instant wealth. Many came from the American goldfields, while others came from China and the

European nations. Although most eventually left the diggings no richer than they arrived, many went on to become successful farmers or traders.

Today Australia supplies much of the western world's iron ore, (mainly from the Pilbara region of Western Australia), bauxite from which aluminium is made, uranium for peaceful purposes, and copper.

Australia also has large reserves of gas, coal and oil and is self-sufficient in these things. However, some special crude oils and their products are still imported.

The most recent venture into world markets is with diamonds which are mined at Lake Argyle near Kununurra in the Kimberley region of Western Australia.

Although Australia is the driest inhabited continent on Earth, careful management of existing water resources has allowed agriculture to become the most important industry. The control of rivers such as the Murray-Darling has brought into production lands that would otherwise be semi-desert. The building of dams such as those of the Snowy Mountains Scheme has allowed hydro-electric power as well as irrigation water to be supplied to many regions.

Because Australia is rich in so many industrial raw materials but has many unique environments, laws protecting both are vitally important. These are drawn up by both the State and Federal Parliaments.

Australia's crust is very rich in minerals.

Australia's food preparation industry has high standards.

Industry

Before Federation in 1901 Australian industry usually served only the colony in which it was based. Tariffs, or customs payments, had to be paid on goods shipped from one colony to another. After Federation free trade was allowed and this helped Australian industry to expand to meet home markets as well as to develop exports.

Today over a million people are involved in manufacturing and the goods produced range from shoes to complex electronic instruments. Shipbuilding and repairing is important to the economy of many States. There are five motor vehicle manufacturers producing cars, trucks and buses mainly for the home market.

Oil refineries supply many of the raw materials to the plastics and chemical industries. These industries in turn produce fertilisers for agriculture, explosives for exploration and mining and a host of components for consumer goods.

Logging — an important but over-exploited industry.

Food processing is one of the most important industries with main exports being dairy products, dried and canned fruits, meat, and drinks such as beers and wines.

Logging and paper supply keep pace with Australia's own needs and while there are strict laws protecting the native forests, Australian hardwoods, such as Ironbark, are in great demand all over the world for building and cabinet work.

Aircraft construction and maintenance is a growing industry and the firms involved are also able to produce weapons such as guided missiles, and to supply world markets with many important aircraft parts.

Cotton and wool producers supply most of the domestic demand for textile manufacture, but a number of man-made fibres are imported.

Trade and Commerce

Australia is the world's major exporter of wool, beef, live sheep and some metals. Agricultural exports make up over 35 per cent of Australia's overseas earnings.

The traditional strong trade links with Europe and the United States of America remain, but over the years Japan and other Asian nations have also become important trading partners. Japan alone takes about 41 per cent of fuel and minerals exported from Australia.

Imports come mainly from the United States of America, followed by Japan and the European Economic Community.

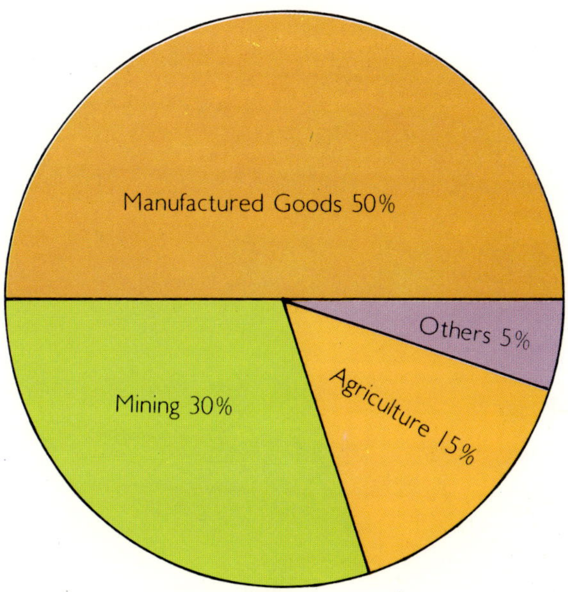

Australia's Main Exports

Transport and Communications

Shipping

Being an island nation, Australia has always relied heavily on ships for world trade. The Australian National Line (ANL) has regular services to ports in Europe, the United States and Asia, and also operates an interstate shipping service carrying raw materials and finished goods in bulk. However, foreign registered vessels are also of major importance to Australian trade.

Modern port facilities with refrigerated stores and container handling equipment serve each State.

Air Transport

The majority of travellers to and from Australia go by air today and Australia's national airline, QANTAS, flies to over 23 countries in the world.

Internal air services are also an important means of transport for both goods and passengers. Many isolated stations and other small communities have their own airstrip and depend on regular commercial flights, or have their own aircraft.

One of the most important air services in Outback Australia is the Flying Doctor Service. Routine and emergency medical aid is provided at all hours through radio links, with home visits and air ambulance services made possible through the use of light aircraft and helicopters. This radio network is also used by many for routine communication. A number of other professionals such as veterinary surgeons also make outback rounds using aircraft.

The modern port of Melbourne is centred around the Yarra River.

City commuters ready to board a train.

Roads and Railways

Australia has over 38,000 kilometres of railway track. Although each State operates its own rail system for internal traffic, the Federal rail system, known as Australian National Railways, also operates services between States. The longest continuous railway in the world crosses the Nullarbor Plain from South Australia to Western Australia.

Australia relies heavily on the trucking industry for the transport of goods. Unlike the railways, the road transport industry is privately owned and operated. Up to 80 per cent of the tonnage of goods carried throughout Australia is carried on trucks.

Communications

Because Australia is so large and has many areas where few people live, there has to be an efficient post and telephone service. Radio communication is also extremely important in the life of many remote communities. Radios can be used to summon medical assistance and to act as a link between students and teachers who provide lessons over the air.

Commercial radio and television services as well as that provided by the Australian Broadcasting Commission (ABC), are available throughout the country.

On outback stations such as Brunette Downs the airstrip is of vital importance.

People and Populations

The 15.5 million people of Australia have many differing backgrounds. The early settlers were mostly British, Irish or German. After World War II, Italians and Greeks came willingly to work in factories, as well as many other citizens from war-torn Europe. Many Asian students study here, and recently refugees from S.E. Asia have added more diversity to our mixed population.

Over three million people live in each of Sydney and Melbourne and close to one million live in each of Brisbane, Adelaide and Perth. In contrast, outback areas only average ten people in every hundred square kilometres.

Refugees

In the past refugees have arrived from countries in eastern Europe such as Hungary, Poland and Czechoslovakia. Others have come from South America. The most recent arrivals have come from South-east Asia, particularly Vietnam, after many years of war. The Australian Government provides assistance to migrants in need, particularly refugees. Accommodation is available in hostels and there are courses in English for those that need them.

Most settle successfully, and several become Australian citizens, but there are many who remain torn between their old country and their new land, and who return when, and if, they can.

The marketplace gathers all nationalities.

Religion

Freedom of religion is an important part of the Australian way of life. The majority of Australians think of themselves as Christians, but others such as Buddhists, Muslims, and Jews all played an important part in the early years of the settlement.

Religious buildings are an attractive feature of Australian towns and cities. They range from tiny churches in small, country communities to the grand city cathedrals. Mosques and synagogues are to be found in all the major cities as well.

Many religious organisations provide community services such as help for the poor, aged, and disabled. Some hospitals and schools belong to, or are run by, churches or other religious foundations.

Festivals

Aboriginal Festivals

In the early years of settlement many missions went to the Aboriginal people to teach them about Christianity. Although even today Christian run missions still exist, the Aboriginal beliefs have survived and are gaining new strength. This is because the stories and festivals associated with their religion belong to the Australian bush and are an important part of helping both blacks and whites to survive in its harsh surroundings. For example, the Aborigines know which are the best routes across a desert or a mountain range because the path was shown to them in the Dreamtime by their ancestral spirits. The same spirits showed them where to find water and food. All this information is passed on to younger generations through songs, dances, stories and paintings.

One of the most famous Aboriginal festivals is the Corroboree, during which songs and dances, often specially composed for the occasion, are performed. The Derby Boab Festival is one such festival which attracts visitors from all over the world.

Chinese New Year

With the many different communities in Australia there are many festivals each year. One of the most popular is the Chinese New Year which is celebrated in Chinese communities all around the country. There is a grand parade led by the dragon dancers. Large numbers of firecrackers are used. The Chinese name their year after a particular animal. 1987, for instance, is the year of the Rabbit.

European festivals

The European settlers brought their own festivals with them and these are mainly Christian. The best known are Christmas, Easter, and New Year and are celebrated at the same time all over the world.

Australian festivals

There are many secular Australian festivals. Agricultural areas host annual Showdays, to promote and test skills of farming life. Rodeos are popular in drier stock areas. Cities also host annual events: Melbourne has Moomba, a carnival of 'floats', concerts and sport; Darwin has a Beercan Raft Derby on the harbour; Alice Springs holds camel races and a dry boat-race; Sydney launches the Sydney-Hobart Yacht Race.

There are also arts festivals in capital cities. The most famous of these takes place in Adelaide once every two years and performers from all over the world are invited. Perth has a Popular Arts festival each February, and in 1986 "Spoleto" came to Melbourne.

An unusual boat-race — The Henley-on-Todd Regatta, Alice Springs.

Architecture

Traditionally the Australian house is of one storey and has a verandah to keep the sun off the walls and so help the inside to stay cool. It is usually built of wood, although mud bricks and pise were often used, and it has a corrugated iron roof.

Many modern houses, however, are built of brick, or brick veneer on a wooden frame and have tiled roofs. Air conditioning is used to keep the inside cool during the hotter summers. Many houses have swimming pools in their gardens.

Within the cities can be found some of the most exciting modern architecture in the world today. Sydney, for example, has its famous Harbour Bridge and the nearby Opera House. Modern high-rise office buildings dominate the skyline of all the major centres and extensive use is made of steel, glass and concrete in their designs.

Inner suburban terraces.

Modern outer suburban houses.

The famous Opera House, Sydney

Education

Education is compulsory and free for all 6–16 year olds. Most children go to State schools, but there are also several fee-paying private schools. Younger children attend kindergarten, or go to pre-school playgroups.

At primary schools students study English, Maths, arts and crafts, computing, physical education, music, science, and social studies. Some also study religion, foreign languages, dance and drama. Special tuition is provided in schools for students from other countries who do not speak English. Many of these students do very well, and later study at one of Australia's 19 universities with their Australian peers. Secondary education is available at high schools or technical colleges for 11–17-year-olds. Apprenticeships and higher technical education can follow, or students may wish to attend a tertiary college or university where specialist training and research facilities are available.

Health and Welfare

Australian health care standards are among the highest in the world. Many new important discoveries have been made in the research departments of hospitals and universities there.

Until recently medical costs were paid for directly by the patient who usually had private health care insurance. Now costs for basic medical treatment are paid for by the Federal Government out of money collected in taxes. People are still free to choose private health care if they prefer it.

Government assistance is provided for disabled people to help them to live independently; and assistance is also given to those who nurse sick relatives at home. If a person cannot work because of illness the law requires them to be paid until they are well enough to work.

Health centres provide free advice for every new mother and child.

The Royal Flying Doctor Service

The Royal Flying Doctor Service is an important medical service to those living in remote areas. The system depends on radio communications and operates out of twelve airfields around the country so that no one is more than about two hours away from professional medical attention. The Service also provides large medical kits to outlying stations and homesteads which can be used under the direction of a doctor through the radio network for vital first-aid treatment in case of injury, or illness. Air ambulances transport emergency cases to main centres for full treatment.

Myths and Legends

The myths and legends of Australia are those of the Aboriginal people and they tell of the creation of the land by the people of the Dreamtime. Each tribe has its own set of stories which are told at certain times.

In the Dreamtime legends, ancestors of the Aborigines often took the form of animals such as eagles, flying foxes, or kangaroos. They left marker stones to show where certain events took place such as battles between tribes, or where people had camped for the night. Often these Dreamtime beings turned into important parts of the landscape such as an isolated range of hills, or a spring of freshwater.

Among these Dreamtime beings the Wandjina figures of the Kimberley area in the far North-west of Australia are perhaps the most mysterious. The paintings of them on the walls of rockcaves are studied by experts from all over the world.

Trail riding is popular with city and country children.

Sport and Recreation

Australia has a perfect climate for a wide range of outdoor pursuits and good sporting facilites are available almost everywhere. These range from the ski-huts and chair lifts for winter sports in the Alps, to large boats for big game fishing offshore.

Organised and Team Sports

Australian sportsmen and women have a high reputation around the world. In the worlds of golf, tennis, athletics, and swimming Australians regularly compete in all the major international competitions. The most famous sporting success of recent years has been the winning of the America's Cup from the Americans who had held it for 132 years. Fremantle became the focus of the sailing world in 1987 as crews and yachts as well as thousands of spectators assembled there for Australia's defence of the world's most famous sailing trophy, and watched America win it back.

Spectator sports such as rugby, cricket and Australian Rules Football have a wide following and many children have an ambition to play for their home team, or to represent their state or country in these and other sports.

Leisure and Recreation

Australians value their leisure time and enjoy outdoor activities, such as bushwalking or camping as a family. There are many special events throughout the year which attract large crowds; these include Steam Rallys, Country Fairs and Agricultural Shows, and in the cities free entertainment is often provided in parks and other spaces.

Eating out is a favourite past-time of many and there are thousands of restaurants which serve food from all over the world. Australians also like to entertain friends at home, especially informally at a Barbecque.

Most States have their own symphony orchestra.

The Arts

Both the State and Federal Government provide funds for all branches of the arts. In recent years the Australian film industry has built up a good reputation with films like *Gallipoli*, *Picnic At Hanging Rock*, and *Breaker Morant*. In the world of opera and music there are many outlets for talented performers: they include State opera companies and many symphony orchestras. A large number of promising young musicians receive support from the Government and may have the opportunity to attend special music camps and training orchestras run by the ABC and other organisations.

The major art galleries hold works by internationally famous painters of Europe, America and Asia, as well as works by modern Australian artists such as John Olsen, Brett Whiteley, Albert Tucker, and Albert Namatjira.

Australia has produced a number of great writers who have won major literary awards. Among these are Patrick White who won the Nobel Prize for Literature in 1973, and Thomas Keneally who was awarded the Booker Prize in 1982. Books by Australian writers for children are sold all over the world and are sometimes made into films, for example *Storm Boy*, by Colin Thiele. Other children's writers include Morris Lurie, Ivan Southall, and Patricia Wrightson.

The Australian Ballet is amongst the best in the world.

Gazetteer

Official name: Commonwealth of Australia
Constitution: Federal Democracy
Head of State: Queen Elizabeth II, represented by the Governor-General
Head of Government: The Prime Minister (Robert Hawke, 1986)
Official language: English
Capital City: Canberra
Area: 7,682,300 sq. km.
Population: 15,280,000
Highest mountain: Mount Kosciusko 2,230 metres
Longest river: Murray Darling
Annual average temperature and rainfall:

	Temperature	*Rainfall*
Sydney	Jan. 22.0°C. July 12.0°C	1181 mm
Brisbane	Jan. 25.0°C. July 14.4°C	1153 mm
Darwin	Jan. 28.3°C. July 25.0°C	1536 mm

Weights and measures: The metric system is used
Currency: One Australian dollar($A) = 100 cents
Airports and shipping: International airports and shipping terminals serve each State.
Agricultural production: The main crops are wheat, barley, fruit, sugarcane. Main livestock are sheep, cattle, pigs, poultry.
Main exports: Metal ores, coal, Textiles, cereals, meat, petroleum and petroleum products
Main imports: Petroleum and petroleum products, road vehicles, industrial machinery, textiles, iron and steel, chemicals, paper
Main trading partners: USA, Japan, UK, Federal Republic of Germany
Treaties and Alliances: Australia is a member of the following international organisations:
The Commonwealth
Organisation for Economic Co-operation and Development (OECD)
ANZUS
The Colombo Plan
The South Pacific Commission
The South Pacific Bureau for Economic Co-operation

Australia's National Anthem: 'Advance Australia Fair'. On royal occasions, 'God Save the Queen' is used

The Australian Flag: The flag of Australia is the British Blue Ensign with a large star beneath the Union Flag, and the five stars of the Southern Cross.

The Australian Coat of Arms: The kangaroo and the emu stand on acacia branches supporting a shield that has the arms of each of the six states on it.

INDEX